Zoo Animals

SNAKES AT THE ZOO

By Seth Lynch

Please visit our website, www.garethstevens.com. For a free color catalog of all our high-quality books, call toll free 1-800-542-2595 or fax 1-877-542-2596.

Library of Congress Cataloging-in-Publication Data

Names: Lynch, Seth, author.
Title: Snakes at the zoo / Seth Lynch.
Description: New York : Gareth Stevens Publishing, [2020] | Series: Zoo animals | Includes index.
Identifiers: LCCN 2018039582| ISBN 9781538239469 (paperback) | ISBN 9781538239483 (library bound) | ISBN 9781538239476 (6 pack)
Subjects: LCSH: Snakes–Juvenile literature. | Zoo animals–Juvenile literature.
Classification: LCC QL666.O6 L845 2020 | DDC 597.96–dc23
LC record available at https://lccn.loc.gov/2018039582

First Edition

Published in 2020 by
Gareth Stevens Publishing
111 East 14th Street, Suite 349
New York, NY 10003

Editor: Therese Shea
Designer: Katelyn E. Reynolds

Photo credits: Cover, p. 1 David Huntley Creative/Shutterstock.com; p. 5 AdaCo/Shutterstock.com; p. 7 Chris Watson/Shutterstock.com; pp. 9, 24 (scales) Sibons photography/Shutterstock.com; p. 11 Mark_Kostich/Shutterstock.com; p. 13 Maria Dryfhout/Shutterstock.com; p. 15 Trahcus/Shutterstock.com; p. 17 Rosa Jay/Shutterstock.com; pp. 19, 24 (python) Yatra/Shutterstock.com; pp. 21, 24 (mamba) NickEvansKZN/Shutterstock.com; p. 23 Dragon Images/Shutterstock.com.

Printed in the United States of America

CPSIA compliance information: Batch #CS19GS: For further information contact Gareth Stevens, New York, New York at 1-800-542-2595.

Contents

I see snakes at the zoo.
I learn a lot!

Snakes have no legs.

Scales cover snake bodies.

Snakes take off old skin.
They grow new skin!

Some snakes have poison.
Most don't.

Snakes eat animals.

There are more than 2,000 kinds of snakes!

The longest is a python.

The fastest is a mamba.

I like the snakes
at the zoo!

Words to Know

mamba

python

scales

Index